# Terry Winters: Printed Works

# Terry Winters: Printed Works

Nan Rosenthal

The Metropolitan Museum of Art, New York

Yale University Press, New Haven and London

This volume is published in conjunction with the exhibition
"Terry Winters: Printed Works," held at The Metropolitan
Museum of Art, New York, from June 12 to September 30, 2001.

This publication is made possible, in part, by the
Roswell L. Gilpatric Fund for Publications.

Published by The Metropolitan Museum of Art
John P. O'Neill, Editor in Chief
Dale Tucker, Editor
Robert Weisberg, Designer and Typesetter
Peter Antony and Sally VanDevanter, Production

All photographs by Eileen Travell, Bruce Schwarz, and
Mark Morosse, The Photograph Studio, The Metropolitan
Museum of Art, except p. 30, by Craig Zammiello.

All works illustrated in this volume are in the collection of
The Metropolitan Museum of Art.

Front cover: *Multiple Visualization Technique,* 1998 (Fig. 22)

Library of Congress Control Number: 2001090014

Separations by Professional Graphics, Inc., Rockford, Illinois
Printed by Brizzolis Arte en Gráficas, Madrid
Bound by Encuadernación Ramos, S.A., Madrid
Printing and Binding coordinated by Ediciones El Viso, S.A., Madrid

# Contents

# Director's Foreword

This exhibition comprises ninety lithographs, etchings, and relief prints by the contemporary painter and draftsman Terry Winters. Drawn entirely from The Metropolitan Museum of Art's collection, it demonstrates the depth of the Museum's holdings in many aspects of modern art and celebrates one of the most versatile artists working today.

Winters's prints first entered the Metropolitan in 1984—only a year after the artist began working in the medium—when what is today the Department of Drawings and Prints acquired three lithographs, the *Morulas*, that Winters had made at the renowned printshop Universal Limited Art Editions (ULAE). Eight years later, that same department acquired *Field Notes*, a portfolio of twenty-five etchings that Winters had just made in Paris at the atelier of Aldo Crommelynck, the great master of intaglio printmaking who produced nearly half of Picasso's graphic oeuvre. In 1998, the Museum's Department of Modern Art acquired two of Winters's abstract oil paintings, *Reflection Line Method* and *Light Source Direction*, both of 1997, as well as four portfolios of prints and a single large etching. This diverse group of works, which includes woodcuts, linoleum cuts, and intaglios, was purchased with funds from the Reba and Dave Williams Gift, a marvelous resource that has allowed the Department of Modern Art to collect prints actively. William S. Lieberman, Jacques and Natasha Gelman Chairman, Department of Modern Art, is well known as a print connoisseur, and he has enthusiastically fostered his department's print acquisitions.

Thus when this exhibition was first conceived several years ago, the Museum already owned sixty-two prints by Winters. Earlier this year, thirty-seven more entered the collection of the Department of Modern Art through a generous gift from Susan Sosnick in memory of her late husband, Robert Sosnick, a Detroit businessman and patron of the arts who was an impassioned collector of Winters's work in all media. This gift—which was strongly supported by Mr. Sosnick's children, Karen Sosnick Schoenberg, Anthony J. Sosnick, and Catherine Sosnick Schwartz—enabled the Museum to turn a planned "in-house" exhibition into a selective but rich retrospective. In addition, seven prints were given to the Museum this year by Robert and Lynda Shapiro and by the artist.

"Terry Winters: Printed Works" was organized by Nan Rosenthal, Consultant in the Department of Modern Art, who has long admired Winters's virtuosity in handling a wide range of print media and who has studied the interaction between the artist's prints and his paintings and drawings. She also wrote the accompanying catalogue, which documents the Museum's exhibition as well as all of Winters's prints made after 1998, when a catalogue raisonné of his prints was completed. The Metropolitan's catalogue is made possible, in part, by the generosity of the Roswell L. Gilpatric Fund for Publications.

*Philippe de Montebello*
*Director, The Metropolitan Museum of Art*

# Acknowledgments

My foremost appreciation goes to Terry Winters for taking the time to answer questions about his prints in The Metropolitan Museum of Art's collection and for his attention to so many details of the exhibition and catalogue. His assistant, Hilary Harp, was an enormous help. From the start of and throughout this project, Bill Goldston of Universal Limited Art Editions (ULAE) has been an enthusiastic supporter, as has Larissa Goldston.

Many colleagues at the Metropolitan have been instrumental in realizing this exhibition. I would like to thank Philippe de Montebello for his support of the catalogue and William S. Lieberman for his dedication to Winters's work and for his wise suggestions about the show. In the Department of Modern Art, I am most grateful to Ida Balboul and Katharine Derosier for expediting many in-house logistics. I also thank Kay Bearman, Lisa M. Messinger, Shirley Levy, Sarah Bergh, Anthony Askin, Cynthia Iavarone, John Koski, Ann Strauser, and former intern Emily Taub. In the Editorial Department, John P. O'Neill, Editor in Chief and General Manager of Publications, has been strongly behind the catalogue from the start, and I am grateful to him. I thank Dale Tucker for his very skillful editing and Robert Weisberg, Peter Antony, and Sally VanDevanter for the design and production of the catalogue.

I thank Mahrukh Tarapor, Associate Director for Exhibitions; Emily K. Rafferty, Senior Vice President for External Affairs; and, in Development, Nina Diefenbach and Kerstin M. Larsen. I am grateful to Linda M. Sylling, Associate Manager for Operations and Special Exhibitions, Daniel Kershaw, Exhibition Designer, and Barbara Weiss, Graphic Designer, for their hard work on the appearance of the exhibition. I also thank George R. Goldner, Drue Heinz Chairman, Department of Drawings and Prints, for lending his department's prints for the exhibition and for the services of his departmental technician, David del Gaizo. I am especially grateful to Samantha Rippner for repeatedly providing expertise about postwar printmaking. I also thank Stella Paul and Elizabeth Hammer-Munemura in Education and Elyse Topalian and Barbara Livenstein in Communications.

I want to express particular gratitude to the family of the late Robert Sosnick—his widow, Susan Sosnick, and his children, Karen Sosnick Schoenberg, Anthony J. Sosnick, and Catherine Sosnick Schwartz—for giving the Metropolitan thirty-seven prints by Winters this year, and to Robert and Lynda Shapiro and Terry Winters for their respective gifts of prints. Finally, I am grateful to Henry B. Cortesi, Jasper Johns, Matthew Marks, Nancy Rosen, Abby Schwartz, Richard Shiff, Richard Solomon, and Hendel Teicher for their assistance in myriad ways.

*N.R.*

# Picturing What We Can't See

**Terry Winters is a consummate New Yorker.**
Highly intelligent and street-smart in a gentle fashion, he
is an avid reader with a wry wit. Winters and his Swiss wife,
Hendel Teicher, a freelance curator and art historian, main-
tain an apartment in Geneva and travel often to museums,
archaeological sites, and centers of craft in Europe, Asia,
and Latin America. Such travel might involve meetings
with the Swiss literary critic and Jean-Jacques Rousseau
scholar Jean Starobinski, whose recent text, *Perfection,
Way, Origin*, Winters interwove with etchings. When
Winters exhibited in Japan in 1989, stops included the
raked temple gardens of Kyoto, an indigo-dye factory, and
a shop selling traditional Japanese woodcutting tools,
some of which Winters felt compelled to acquire. These
visits played into the creation of two portfolios of relief
prints in this exhibition, *Furrows* (1989) and *Glyphs*
(1995). Unquestionably, travel feeds Winters's art.

The focal space of Winters's artistic activity, however, consists of several stair-linked floors in a building
in the lower Manhattan neighborhood of Tribeca. Here
Winters has a large painting studio on one level and, on
another level, a spacious studio for drawing and an office
with many countertops and a computer. Winters's living
spaces on these floors weave privately above and below
the studios. They abound with stunning artifacts from
widely different cultures, sensuously sculptural plants,
out-of-the-ordinary contemporary furniture, and many
books. Two sleek, honey brown Abyssinian cats share their
space with small reproductions of their aloof Egyptian
ancestors. The atmosphere is homey, humorous, and
elegant, yet resolutely resists shelter magazine chic.

The other centers of Winters's artistic activity are
two: there are the drawings in many materials—for
example, gouache, watercolor, juicy crayon, graphite,
charcoal, and fine-lined ink—that he makes not only at
home but almost whenever and wherever he travels;
and then there are the distinguished printmaking ateliers
where he has worked regularly for the past nineteen
years, producing more than 150 lithographs, intaglios,
woodcuts, linoleum cuts, and screenprints. Ninety of

Figure 1. **Morula III,** 1983 – 84

these have been selected for this retrospective. A catalogue raisonné of Winters's prints from 1982 to 1998 contains an astute narrative by Richard H. Axsom about Winters's development as a printmaker over much of this period.[1] The Metropolitan's catalogue documents the contents of the Museum's exhibition as well as Winters's entire print production subsequent to the publication of the catalogue raisonné in 1999.

This essay examines Winters's recent prints, but it also looks back at earlier works that forecast his current focus: to propose visually, through his essentially abstract art, how the world at present is linked in ways we cannot always visualize but constantly experience. With respect to this pursuit, Winters sometimes refers to the term "cyberspace," coined by William Gibson in his 1984 science fiction novel *Neuromancer.*[2] Gibson's popular neologism derives from the word cybernetics, which M.I.T. mathematician Norbert Wiener created in 1948 to describe the branch of science dealing with the comparative study of human control systems, such as the brain and nervous system, and complex electronic systems. (Cybernetics, in turn, derives from the Greek noun *kybernetes*, or helmsman, which is from the verb *kybernao*, meaning to steer or to govern.) Winters is as interested in brain function and the structure of neural connections as he is in images of cybergeography he has found on the Internet. Asked recently what Gibson's term cyberspace really means, Winters replied: "I don't know *exactly*, but one classic definition is the place you go when you're on the telephone. It's the informational space out there. It's not immaterial but incorporeal. I'm interested in how to give a picture of these things we can't see."[3]

This is a very different ambition for abstract art than that of the late Symbolism of Odilon Redon and Wassily Kandinsky or the structured utopianism of Piet Mondrian, all of which have at times interested Winters. It is closer to the diagrammatic abstraction developed by Marcel Duchamp and Francis Picabia and to the tradition of American Abstract Expressionist painting, to which the vigor of Winters's often gestural touch relates. In some respects, Winters's trajectory from organic imagery in the early 1980s to complex, more purely abstract webs in his present work in various two-dimensional media has parallels in the development of Abstract Expressionist art. Jackson Pollock, Mark Rothko, and Barnett Newman, among others, moved from biomorphic Surrealist forms in the 1930s and early to mid-1940s to pure abstraction soon after that.

Figure 2. **Double Standard,** 1984

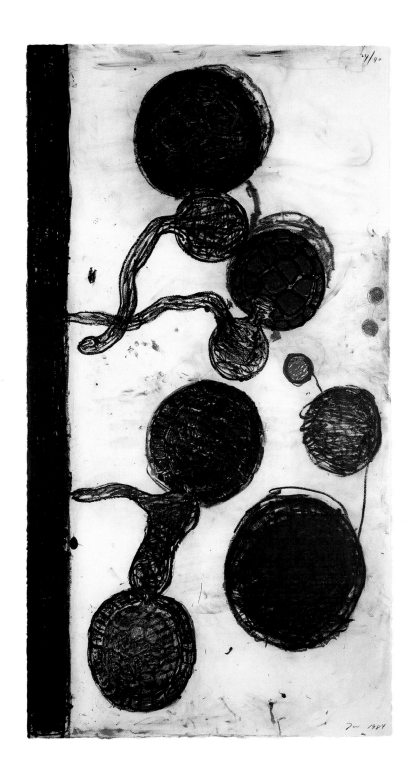

Winters was born in 1949 and grew up in Brooklyn, for the first decade of his life in Brownsville, then a large lower-middle-class Jewish community, and later in the slightly more upscale neighborhoods of Midwood and Flatbush. His father worked in construction and later managed real estate properties. One of his father's constructions was a linoleum floor, made for Winters's bedroom, that contained scalloped cutouts of cowboys and Indians. The artist recalled his connection to this material much later when making the linoleum cuts *Glyphs.*

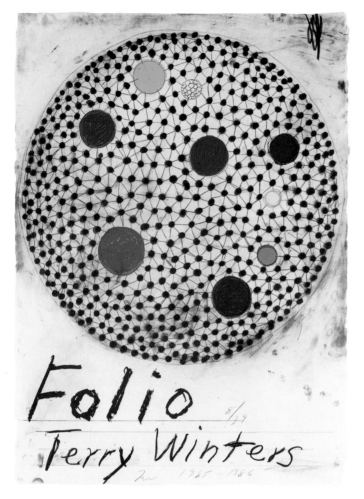

Figure 3. **Folio, Title Page,** 1985–86

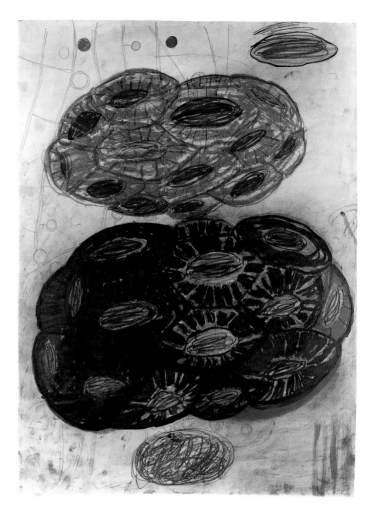

Figure 4. **Folio Four,** 1985–86

From his preschool days Winters loved to draw. He remembers that his parents were "remarkably supportive" when, in junior high school, he became serious about a professional involvement in the visual arts. He submitted his portfolio to one of New York's public high schools with competitive admissions, the High School of Art and Design on Second Avenue between 56th and 57th Street in Manhattan. Known then, as it is now, as a school of commercial art, it had the advantage for Winters, who was commuting from Brooklyn, of being thirty minutes closer to home than the perhaps more obvious choice, the High School of Music and Art, which was farther north.

In addition to a full load of academic classes, at Art and Design there was also a program of required art courses. Winters managed to persuade the administration that instead of taking commercial art, he would stick mainly to painting, sculpture, and drawing.

After school and on Saturdays, Winters and a friend discovered the wider free culture of the 57th Street art galleries: from Mondrian, Abstract Expressionism, and Pop at Sidney Janis to the latest contemporary art at Leo Castelli's 77th Street space. There, because of his persistent visits, Winters was invited into the back rooms to see works not on public view. In this way, Winters, even though he was a young teenager, experienced the extraordinary excitement of art in New York in the 1960s.

During this time Winters regularly visited the city's museums. At the Museum of Modern Art, he not only saw painting and sculpture by European modernists, including Surrealists such as Joan Miró, and work by American Abstract Expressionists, but he also looked with equal curiosity at exhibitions of architecture and design and at the rotating shows of modern prints and drawings, where he first encountered the graphic work of Jasper Johns and Robert Rauschenberg. Some of his memories—of frequently visiting the exhibition of Edvard Munch's paintings and prints at the Guggenheim Museum in 1965–66, and of seeing the Metropolitan's oil by Willem de Kooning, *Easter Monday* (1955–56), hanging near Rauschenberg's giant collage painting *Rebus* (1955), then on loan to the Museum—remain vivid.

Following high school Winters moved to Crosby Street in SoHo and commuted in reverse to the Pratt Institute, in the Clinton Hill section of Brooklyn, from which he graduated with a Bachelor of Fine Arts in 1971. Living on Crosby Street, near the secondhand bookstores that were then a rich resource on Fourth Avenue and lower Broadway, encouraged his habit of buying books, especially volumes with illustrated natural histories or other kinds of scientific imagery. Technically, Winters majored in fine art at Pratt, although he took a wide variety of courses there, including several in industrial design and architecture, and for a time he considered becoming an architect. Although he decided against it, his fascination with structures has been ongoing and is frequently expressed in his drawings, paintings, and prints. From the attention Winters pays to the appearance of the actual portfolios that house many of his prints, it is evident that he acquired an expertise in graphic design as well. While at Pratt, he also audited courses at the School of Visual Arts in Manhattan, where a number of artists roughly a decade older than Winters, such as the sculptor Richard Serra, were teaching

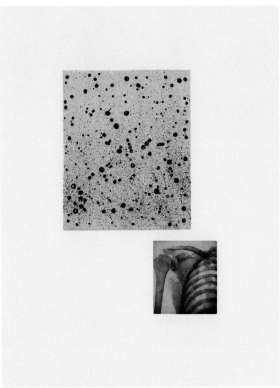

Figures 5, 6. **Fourteen Etchings 2** and **Fourteen Etchings 6,** 1989

Figure 7. **Novalis,** 1983 – 89

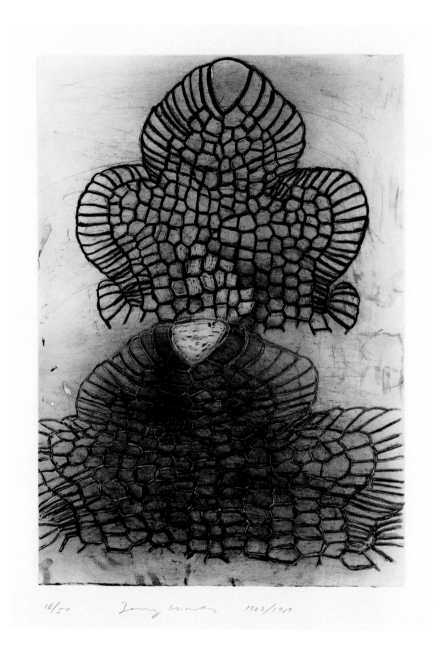

16/50    Terry Winters    1583/1989

part-time and rethinking the poignantly spare Minimalist style that led advanced art during the mid-1960s.

To support himself as a young artist, Winters took various jobs, including construction and picture framing. Through the latter he learned a good deal about techniques of handling papers: how to hinge them, how to cut mats, as well as how to build frames. And he painted and drew, gradually, over almost a decade, accumulating work he decided to exhibit. After showing paintings and drawings in several group shows in the late 1970s and early 1980s, in 1982 he had his first one-artist exhibition of paintings and drawings at the Sonnabend Gallery in New York. By that time his paintings had evolved from nearly monochrome, Minimalist compositions with a painterly facture into what is confusingly termed organic abstraction. Based in part

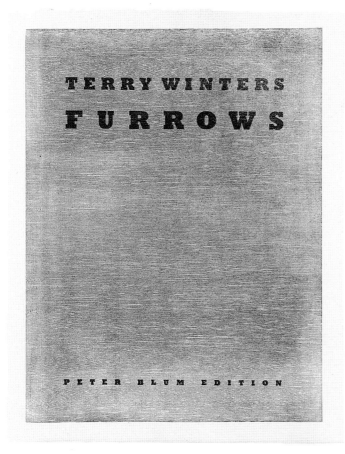

Figure 8. **Furrows,** title page, 1989

Figure 9. **Furrows IV,** 1989

on his notebook sketches of botanical, zoological, and architectural forms, including the skeletal tension and compression structures of Buckminster Fuller and Frei Otto, these new paintings also contained distinct allusions to specific forms in nature. Yet they were not representational in any traditional sense. There was no local color, and, for the most part, individual forms did not relate to one another so as to create either an illusion of depth or a classically balanced composition. Frequently Winters's virtuoso applications of paint straight from the tube vied on the same canvas with fine graphic lines and scratches in the painted surface. Forms microscopic in the natural world were often hugely enlarged, giving them a forceful physical presence.

Some of Winters's earliest prints, for example, the large lithographs *Morula I, II,* and *III* (Fig. 1), show spherical masses of fertilized ova at the stage of embryonic growth when more and more segmentation takes place, eventually leading to organ development. Biologists term this stage morula, from the Latin word for mulberry, because the segmentation resembles that berry's distinctive aggregate structure. Winters was not trying to illustrate cell division but rather was thinking about embryology as a kind of mythology, perhaps about the genesis of complex spaces. The segmented spheres, built mostly in several velvety blacks with greasy French litho crayons, float in an indeterminate space, while finer marking materials, such as pencils, established much smaller, delicate forms, including the mulberry itself, near the margins of the sheets. One result of this was to call attention to the texture of the paper the lithographs

Figure 10. **Section,** 1991

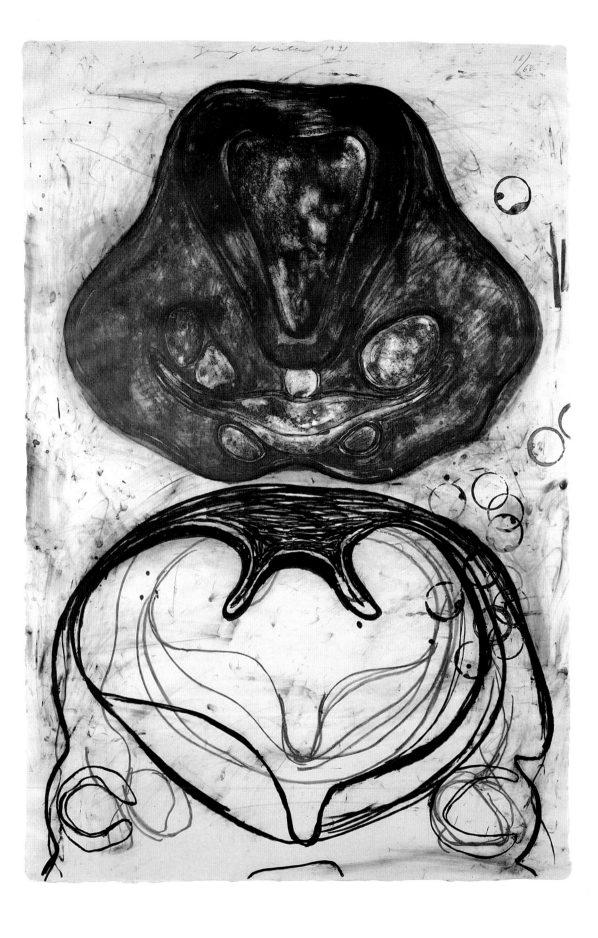

were printed on and thus also to the physical surface of the print.

Shortly before Winters's exhibition in 1982, Bill Goldston, coprincipal and manager of Universal Limited Art Editions (ULAE) in West Islip, New York, had been struck by the quality of Winters's drawings and later that year invited the artist to make lithographs at ULAE. Curiously, despite the variety of courses he had taken in high school and at Pratt, Winters at that point had never made a print. ULAE, founded in 1957 by Tatyana Grosman, was by then renowned for having revived an interest in printmaking among notable American painters and sculptors and particularly for fostering intense collaborations among the artists and the printers. The ULAE printers responded patiently and imaginatively to what the artists wanted to do, and the printers became expert at converting commercial printing techniques, such as offset lithography, into processes viable for fine art. Winters began going to ULAE on a weekly basis; the then small shops at West Islip became a kind of extension of his own studio.

In addition to collaborating with Goldston, whose ongoing enthusiasm undoubtedly encouraged his rapid progress as a printmaker, Winters worked closely at ULAE with printers of his own generation, including Keith Brintzenhofe, John Lund, and Craig Zammiello. Together with Goldston, they developed various ways for Winters to draw directly on paper and then for these images to be transferred to the litho stone or metal plate. This was achieved not with transfer paper but with solvents or ghosting techniques that registered the texture of the drawing paper and also avoided Winters's having to laboriously copy his own images or work in reverse. Winters would then continue to draw his images directly on the stone or plate. From the start Winters went to the shop with drawings he had prepared earlier, a practice he has continued wherever he makes prints.

Winters's ambition for prints became clear in 1984 with *Double Standard* (Fig. 2), a 6½-by-3½-foot lithograph

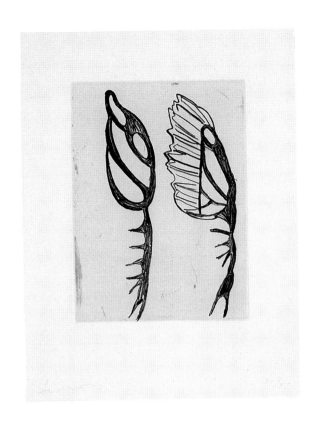

Figures 11, 12. **Field Notes, 1** and **Field Notes, 19,** 1992

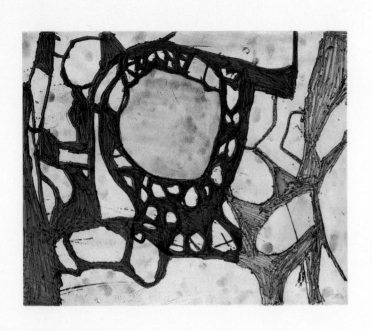

Figure 13. **Models for Synthetic Pictures, 1,** 1994

that continued the cellular imagery of the *Morula* series and extended it with plantlike tendrils. The following year, he embarked on his first print portfolio in order to combine into one unified work a range of images that had been occurring in his recent drawings and paintings. *Folio* (Figs. 3, 4) comprises eleven lithographs, beginning with a title page on which a bouncy orb, reminiscent of a Buckminster Fuller geodesic dome, encompasses smaller, gumball-like circles in primary and secondary colors. The concluding colophon page contains the printer's "draw downs," or tests, of the twenty-three colors of ink used for the portfolio. The nine prints in between were made in part with vintage carbonized lithography ink and on J. Whatman paper from the 1950s, which was sized to receive the inks in very specific ways that Winters liked. The sheets combine the delicacy of his pencil marks and faint smudges on the plates with a strong range of blacks. Writing in 1971 about De Kooning's black-and-white lithographs, which had impressed Winters, the poet John Ashbery described De Kooning's being happy "to conjugate the nuances of black—crisp or velvety, thin or gooey—with a virtuoso's relish."[4] In the *Folio* lithographs Winters does something similar, although his loose but structured lines are utterly different from De Kooning's broad swaths. Several of the sheets, for example, *Folio Three*, anticipate the fields of nets in Winters's recent work.

After *Folio*, a great many of Winters's prints have been published in portfolio form. He came to believe that prints occupy a space within his work equal to that of any other medium; for him, there is no hierarchy that

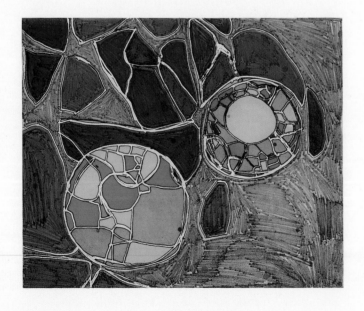

Figure 14. **Models for Synthetic Pictures, 9,** 1994

positions painting and drawing above prints. Winters likes to refer to Barnett Newman's introduction to his *18 Cantos* of 1963–64, in which Newman states that lithography "is not a poor man's substitute for painting or for drawing. Nor a . . . translation of something from one medium into another. . . . it is an instrument that one plays. It is like a piano or an orchestra; and as with an instrument, it *interprets.*" [5] Winters extends this point, extolling the great variety of intensities that different media, including different print media, make available to the artist.

Winters had already experimented briefly with etching at ULAE when he was commissioned by the New York print publisher Ilene Kurtz to work in Paris with the legendary intaglio printer Aldo Crommelynck. After World War II, Crommelynck had worked with many of the eminent School of Paris painters. He was Picasso's etcher in the south of France during the artist's last decades and printed nearly half of his graphic oeuvre. By the time Winters met him, Crommelynck had also worked with distinguished American and British printmakers such as Jasper Johns and Richard Hamilton.

Crommelynck is a master of classical etching techniques who—in part because of his skill in preparing plates—is particularly known for the nuances he can enable an artist to achieve with the continuous tonal areas of aquatint and the finely drawn lines of soft-ground etching. Other than an intense work ethic, ULAE—with its informal and experimental atmosphere, communal lunches, and considerable humor—could not be more different from Crommelynck's atelier, which occupies two levels of a nineteenth-century building that is within a gated courtyard in Paris's elegant seventh arrondissement. Crommelynck's shop is austere and, for a visitor, rather intimidating despite the printer's cordiality, modesty, and intelligence. Winters's first portfolio printed at Crommelynck's, a suite of nine intaglios titled *Album* that he made during several two-week visits, was published in 1988 and contains imagery closely related to that in the

Figure 15. **Glyphs, 6,** 1995

19

*Folio* lithographs. He returned several years later to make a portfolio of twenty-five intaglios, *Field Notes* (Figs. 11, 12), which was published by Crommelynck in 1992. The *Field Notes* were deliberately small works, each printed on one plate and in one black ink, with a range of imagery that related in part to new paintings Winters was working on following his midcareer retrospective at the Whitney Museum in 1991. Winters used the opportunity to learn from Crommelynck's encyclopedic knowledge of intaglio techniques, from hard-ground and open-bite etching to scraping to various methods of manipulating aquatint with sugar lift and spit bite.

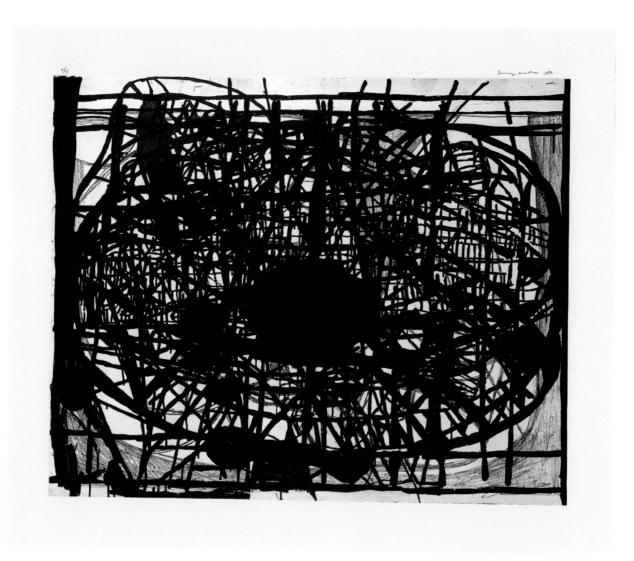

Figure 16. **Systems Diagram,** 1996

20

In these same years Winters was also working on intaglios at ULAE, beginning with the unusual 1989 portfolio *Fourteen Etchings.* Except for the first page, two plates were used for each sheet. The photogravures on the lower right portion of the pages were made from photographs of X rays of human anatomical parts. These images were taken from a volume by Wilhelm Röntgen (who discovered X rays in 1895) that Winters found on one of his second-hand-bookstore scavenger hunts. They proceed roughly in order going down the skeleton, from a skull in *Fourteen Etchings 2* (Fig. 5) to a foot in *Fourteen Etchings 14.* To the upper middle of each sheet, Winters glued separate printed sheets with different images, from concentric circles in *Fourteen Etchings 2,* which echo the cranium and eye sockets in the photogravure, to a celestial map in *Fourteen Etchings 6* (Fig. 6). These glued sheets began as drawings on Mylar, which were made into photogravures that Winters then reworked with aquatint. He

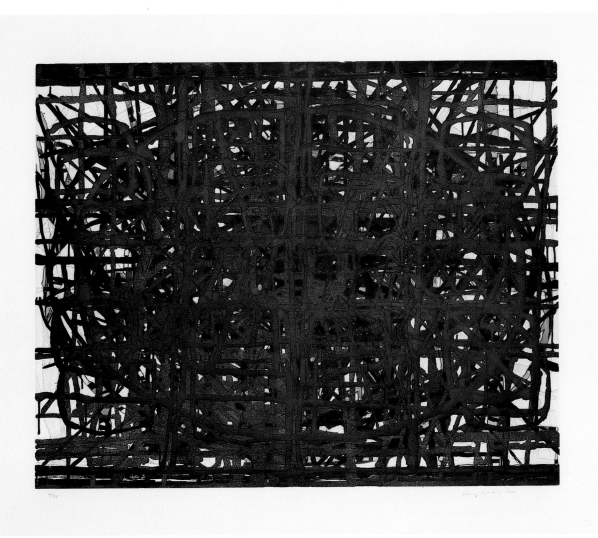

Figure 17. **Internal and External Values,** 1998

introduced the portfolio with a typeset alphabetical list of the Latin and English names of the major constellations.[6]

In 1989, commissioned by the New York print publisher Peter Blum, Winters embarked on his first relief prints, the five woodcuts *Furrows* (Figs. 8, 9). He made them at the mountaintop atelier of François Lafranca in the Lepontine Alps of Ticino, an Italian-speaking canton of southeastern Switzerland. Undoubtedly aware of expressive woodcuts by Paul Gauguin and Edvard Munch in which

the imprint of the grain of the wood is an important component of the image, Winters both exploited and complicated that tradition to make highly elegant works in which the technology used is not immediately apparent.

The *Furrows* sheets were each printed from two different blocks of wood using a dark gray etching ink; the transparency of the ink was enhanced to make the grains of the woods particularly visible. Winters drew and carved his imagery on blocks of mahogany, a very hard

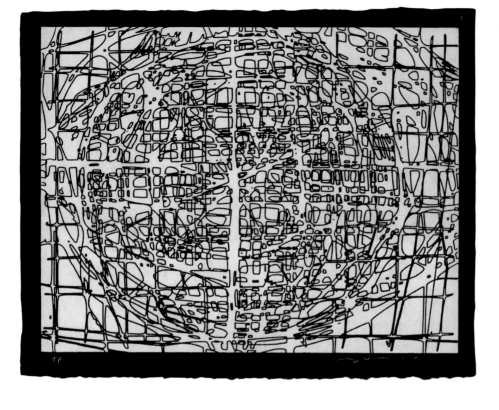

Figure 18. **Graphic Primitives, 1,** 1998

22

Figure 19. **Graphic Primitives, 6,** 1998

wood. He used traditional woodworking tools he had just bought in Japan to pull, rather than gouge, grooves of curving parallel lines away from the mahogany planks. The lighter lines on the prints show what he removed from the blocks; the darker areas were left in relief, received ink, and were printed. He worked on the mahogany blocks so that when they were printed, the grain of the wood would run horizontally. He then took the printed sheets of paper and printed them again using inked, uncarved oak planks on which the grains ran vertically. One result on the final sheets is a kind of moiré pattern formed by the meshing of the two directionally different wood grains.

Winters's imagery in *Furrows* derives in part from illustrations he had examined of cross sections of the cranial nervous system. As mentioned earlier, brain connections interest Winters at least as much as connections made in cyberspace, and he was intrigued by the way the extended patterns of the nervous system build into an overall structure. Recently returned from Kyoto, Winters was also thinking about the temple gardens of raked pebbles and sand he had just visited, in which parallel curving lines—which might be described as furrows—exhibit a kind of beauty that is systemic but that also shows traces of the gardener's patterning hand. Moreover, in *Furrows* Winters wanted to produce a family of structures that resonated with the layers of the wood grain, the annual rings that are indexes of growth and of the passage of time.

In 1994, ULAE published another portfolio of Winters's intaglios, the twelve startling *Models for Synthetic Pictures* (Figs. 13, 14). They related to ink and pencil drawings Winters had been working on for the preceding two years. In a deliberate departure from earlier imagery that Winters felt had been locked into naturalistic readings, he turned to brilliantly colored, complex fields of imaginary curved and sometimes angular forms within forms that are bound and intricately connected by outlines, almost like cloisonné enamel. With a perhaps ironic but also heartfelt quotation from the mature painting of

Mondrian, Winters set up a program for the series using only five plates: two with black inks and one each in red, yellow, and blue. The linear outlines of shapes on the copperplates of the etchings were initially established by pen markers filled with lacquer. The lacquer stopped the etching acid from biting the plate where the forms were outlined. This enabled Winters first to draw directly on the plate and then to react to proofs of the drawn plates with aquatint applications of the primary color inks within the drawn outlines. These areas were sometimes toned with further applications of red, yellow, and blue that modified their intensities; the prints were also extended with hatchings of pencil lines etched in soft ground.

Within the dark blue silk portfolio Winters designed to house the *Models for Synthetic Pictures*, he included three extra sheets that point to his limitation of his palette to black and the primaries: a title page with black type on a cobalt blue rectangle; a colophon page with black type on chrome yellow; and a third page, with black type on a cadmium red rectangle, that contains twelve recondite meditations on elements of picture making. Winters pointed out recently that at the time he "was interested in how synthetic the pictures felt and how they were loaded with references to one's experience of things and how they occurred in the world. I was taking information from lots of different sources and feeding it into the process of improvising a new imagery. I was beginning to think that the kinds of images I was building had, rather than a representational relationship to the world, a kind of isomorphic relationship." He added, however, that "the images existed in complex illusionistic spaces."

The following year Winters produced a significant short book, *Ocular Proofs* (New York: The Grenfell Press, 1995). It contains loosely rendered webs of black ink lines. Many of these lines are diagonal, yet many of the images are centered by a strong vertical element. Although the drawings indicate intricate structures, they do not connote architecture or reflect plans of any existing or imagined

Figure 20. **Set of Ten, 2 of 10,** 1998

Figure 21. **Set of Ten, 6 of 10,** 1998

urban spaces. Opposite each drawing is a poetic paragraph by Winters about picture making. One, "Regions," could be a description of the stained-glass-like print *Models for Synthetic Pictures, 9* (Fig. 14):

> the painted world is a wavelength of variable images in visible light/colored filters give a completely new window on the scene/each spectral region provides a regime, an independent observational realm/in addition, within each spectral dimension, pictures are obtained/in more dramatic examples, light appears to spiral out from a central disk/the luminous arms are regions of the spectrum/evolution produces the helical painting/pictures can change knowledge of systems forever

For an artist whose interest in the virtual world of information systems, computer visualization, and cyberspace was growing rapidly, the assertion that "pictures can change knowledge of systems forever" is an existential one. It seems to say that the actuality of a single concrete object, such as a painting or print made freely by an insightful individual, is at least equal to the virtuality of an entire system or set of abstract concepts. Winters was confirming his belief that thought is linked closely to form, and that consciousness and its products, such as abstract painting, can produce as "natural" a depiction of the world as that in the mythological stories of a classical Greek drama.[7]

That same year Winters returned to making relief prints with *Glyphs* (Fig. 15), a portfolio of six linoleum

Figure 22. **Multiple Visualization Technique,**
1998

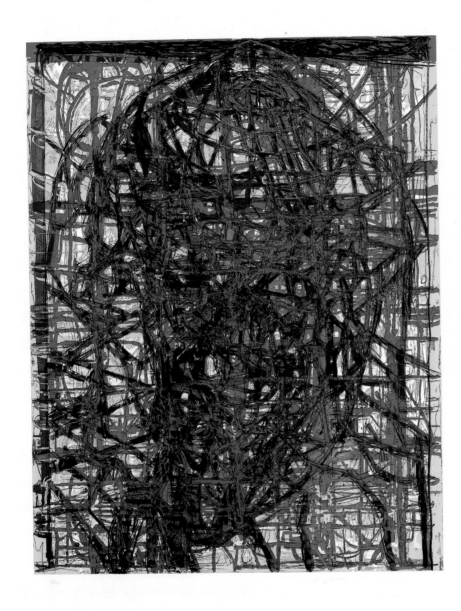

cuts printed by Leslie Miller at the Grenfell Press. In
contrast to the coloristic complexity of the *Models for
Synthetic Pictures* etchings, the spiderweb forms in the
*Glyphs* are on very thin, delicate white Japanese paper
in just two colors, black and indigo. As his imagery was

becoming more complex and, in his term, "technological,"
Winters was interested in the idea of subjecting this graphic
complexity to what he regarded as the most childlike of
printing techniques, "one step above potato prints." First
he cut away his drawings on the butter-soft linoblock, a

Figure 23. **Linking Graphics,**
2000

surface distinctly easier to work than the mahogany of *Furrows*—an advantage that might have encouraged the lively complexity of the lines. Areas left in relief were printed with a black oil ink; then, following a linocut technique conceived by Picasso in the early 1960s called *épreuves rincées* (rinsed proofs), Winters had the entire sheets rinsed with a water-based indigo dye. The dye adhered only to the cutaway areas left blank on the white paper and not to the black-inked relief areas. Where the oily black ink and water-based blue dye met, they repulsed one another, and a slight halo effect was created. This gave these prints some of their extraordinary vitality, as did Winters's combining the tissue-like paper and the subtle indigo with assertive, abstract pictographs.[8]

During the second half of 1995 and early 1996, Winters made 125 ink-on-paper drawings, each $8\frac{1}{4}$ by $11\frac{5}{8}$ inches, called the *Computation of Chains*. These graphic studies became source material for an enormous body of work he produced over the next five years, including large paintings in oil and alkyd resin on linen that were shown in Europe and at the Matthew Marks Gallery in New York in 1997 and 1999; five large individual but related etchings made at ULAE between 1996 and 1998; and a portfolio of smaller etchings, the *Set of Ten* (Figs. 20, 21), begun at ULAE in 1998 and made to accompany a text by Jean Starobinski. (Winters later made twenty-eight additional etchings for the Starobinski project, which were bound in a book with the translated text and published, together with the *Set of Ten*, as *Perfection, Way, Origin*, 2001.) Works derived from the *Computation of Chains* drawings also include a portfolio of relief prints, the nine woodcuts *Graphic Primitives* (Figs. 18, 19), made in 1998 with David Lasry at Two Palms Press in New York.

Much of the essential syntax of these works—from the original drawings to the large paintings (for example, two oils in the collection of the Metropolitan, *Reflection Line Method* and *Light Source Direction*, both of 1997), as well as the prints, some of which influenced the paintings—involves loosely structured grids crossed by diagonals and encircled by elliptical lines. The lines narrow and thicken, often in a gestural manner; the webs that they create are layered in such a way as to suggest a deep, indeterminate space.

In contrast to the works of the 1980s that first established Winters's reputation, which contain relatively discrete if occasionally merging objects inhabiting an undifferentiated field, these new works are themselves fields. The fields extend both across the surface of the picture and into depth. In the paintings, the depth is created partly by changes in color and by contrasts between the thick and thin networks of lines, as well as by the viewer's awareness that these works have been constructed in layers. At the same time, Winters's impasto application of paint and his loose handling of geometry consistently lure the viewer's eye to the surface of the works.

The five large etchings related to *Computation of Chains* are each printed in one color of ink and on one plate. Here the etching process itself—that is, the successive bites of the copperplate made by various techniques, such as sugar-lift aquatint, which enables the artist to draw brushstrokes on the plate—helps to build a sense of depth. In the earliest of these etchings, *Systems Diagram* of 1996 (Fig. 16), faint pencil lines made with soft-ground etching also create depth toward the lower corners of the print. The abstract imagery of the print is fluid and appears to be in motion, perhaps because there are many elliptical marks. Yet it is bordered by strong vertical lines at the sides that freeze the frame of the image. In other etchings in the group, the "freeze-frame" effect (the term is Winters's) is achieved with thicker horizontal lines at the top and bottom of the field. This occurs in *Internal and External Values* of 1998 (Fig. 17), the last of the five etchings and the only one printed not in black but in Prussian blue ink. This ink has the capacity to receive different levels of etching on the plate in different tones, some richly opaque, others paler and almost transparent. In this way the color itself helps to establish the complex depth in the print. Winters further complicated the gridded fields with more emphatic ellipses in another print of 1998, *Multiple Visualization Technique* (Fig. 22), a large vertical etching made from four plates in four colors: yellow, red, blue, and black. Despite the strong ovals, this print contains echoes of Mondrian's oil *Broadway Boogie-Woogie* (1942–43).

In several ways the various paintings and prints derived from Winters's *Computation of Chains* drawings may be understood as metaphors of cyberspace or as maps of the informational space we experience but cannot see. Making works as dependent on gesture and on varieties of pressure and touch as these, Winters became interested in what an image without the benefit of the inflection of his touch might look like. Accordingly, to make the relief prints *Graphic Primitives* (Figs. 18, 19), a portfolio of nine woodcuts completed in 1998, he scanned some of the *Computation of Chains* drawings into a computer. This produced images in which the lines were distinctly even and crisp compared to those in almost all of his other work. Winters used a graphics program in a computer to layer areas, change the scale of shapes, and play with composition. A disk of the computer-manipulated images was sent to a machinist, who incised them with a laser onto blocks of cherry wood, and the blocks were used to print the woodcuts. Winters returned to Picasso's rinsed-proof method to produce the final sheets; the areas left

Figure 24. **Amplitude,** 2000

28

in relief on the cherry wood were rolled with white oil ink and printed on white paper. The entire sheet was then rinsed with black Sumi ink, and the incised areas—the drawings—printed in black, as did the substantial deckle-edged borders of the paper. Like the blurry, hand-made profiles of some of Barnett Newman's zips, the deckle edges counter the crispness of the drawn imagery.

Winters has for some time been interested in the writings of the French philosopher Gilles Deleuze—for example, in Deleuze's metaphor of the rhizome, a plant growth system in which stemlike strands spread horizontally but also extend shoots above and roots below. Deleuze uses the rhizome to exemplify the absence of hierarchy in the contemporary world, where there is no longer a path from God above to humanity below but rather a network within which you may take an infinite number of paths to get from point a to point b. Winters's most recent prints and paintings seem informed by his readings of Deleuze, especially *The Fold: Leibniz and the Baroque*,[9] and by looking at the way computer animation can morph space. For example, *Amplitude* (Fig. 24), a large vertical intaglio in four colors, and *Pattern* (2001), a similarly tall lithograph and digital print, both made at ULAE, consist of interwoven systems of meshwork that build and torque space. In contrast to most of the imagery of the previous five years, the wire-frame-like structures that twist through these works appear to have the capacity to extend beyond the perimeters of the sheet. No borders except those of the plate or paper stop these images from growing in all directions, rhizomelike, into the world we cannot see. In this respect Winters's work connects to the infinitely interconnected realm of cyberspace; at the same time, however, it also echoes a tradition at some variance with the world of the Internet: Abstract Expressionist painting.

## Notes

1. Richard H. Axsom, "The Philosophers' Stone: The Prints of Terry Winters," in Nancy Sojka with Nancy Watson Barr, *Terry Winters Prints 1982–1998: A Catalogue Raisonné* (Detroit: The Detroit Institute of Arts, 1999), pp. 11–36.

2. Winters believes that Gibson's writing was influenced by William Burroughs's hallucinatory montage novel *Naked Lunch* (1959) and Burroughs's fiction from the 1960s and 1970s involving time travel and telepathy.

3. Unless otherwise noted, quotations from Terry Winters come from the author's interviews with the artist on December 13, 2000, and January 18, 2001.

4. John Ashbery, "Willem de Kooning," *Art News Annual*, no. 37 (1971), p. 126.

5. Barnett Newman, "Preface to *18 Cantos*," in *Barnett Newman: Selected Writings and Interviews*, ed. John P. O'Neill (New York: Alfred A. Knopf, 1990), p. 184.

6. Winters took the constellation names from the fourth edition of *Roget's International Thesaurus*. *Fourteen Etchings* was initially inspired by Winters's reading of Edgar Allan Poe's philosophical prose poem "Eureka" (1848), in which Poe writes about the universe as a system of interdependent parts. The ironies and mysticism in Poe's poem and the poem's relation to Winters's portfolio are discussed in David Shapiro, "Terry Winters: Symbolism and Its Discontents," in *Terry Winters: Fourteen Drawings/Fourteen Etchings*, exh. cat. (Munich: Galerie Jahn und Fusban, 1990).

7. Winters discusses related issues in Clifford S. Ackley, "Terry Winters and Cliff Ackley: A Conversation," *Art New England* 14 (June –July 1993), pp. 29–31.

8. Winters first encountered Picasso's rinsed-proof linoleum cuts in a traveling exhibition at the Brooklyn Museum in 1984, "Picasso the Printmaker: Graphics from the Marina Picasso Collection," organized by Steven A. Nash for the Dallas Museum of Art. The accompanying catalogue contained an extensive text by the cataloguer of Picasso's graphic work, Brigitte Baer, whom Winters later met and talked with at Crommelynck's atelier in Paris.

9. Gilles Deleuze, *The Fold: Leibniz and the Baroque*, trans. Tom Conley (Minneapolis: University of Minnesota Press, 1992).

Terry Winters at Universal Limited Art Editions (ULAE), Bayshore,
New York, 2001. Photograph by Craig Zammiello

# Works in the Exhibition

Dimensions are in inches, followed by centimeters; height precedes width. All works are in the collection of The Metropolitan Museum of Art.

## Catalogue Raisonné Numbers

Reference numbers (e.g., Sojka 16) are provided for all works published in Nancy Sojka's 1999 catalogue raisonné of Winters's prints. Full cataloging data is given for all prints produced subsequent to publication of the catalogue raisonné. Works marked with an asterisk (*) are not in the exhibition but have been included here because they were produced subsequent to the catalogue raisonné.

## Edition Numbers and Proofs

Edition numbers (e.g., 16/20) refer to the prints in the Museum's collection.

AP: Artist's proof (impression printed for the artist and excluded from the numbering of an edition but exactly like the edition in every other respect)

PP: Printer's or publisher's proof (impression printed for the printers or publishers and excluded from the numbering of an edition but exactly like the edition in every other respect)

BAT: Bon à tirer (proof approved by the artist that establishes the standard for the edition)

TP: Trial proof (test proof that differs in appearance from the edition)

WP: Working proof (test proof incorporating additions by hand or other means that reflect experimentation with the development of the image)

Signing proof: Proof made to test placement of the signature

## Portfolios

Cataloging data common to all prints in a portfolio is provided in the general entry for the portfolio; data specific to a particular print is given in that print's individual entry.

*Morula I,* 1983–84
Lithograph printed in two colors on Japanese handmade Toyoshi paper (torn to size)
Sheet (irregular): $41\frac{3}{4}$ x $31\frac{5}{8}$ (106 x 80.3)
Signed (TW) and dated (1983–84), upper right
Numbered (30/38), upper left
Printers: Keith Brintzenhofe and Thomas Cox
Publisher: Universal Limited Art Editions (ULAE), West Islip, New York
Stewart S. MacDermott Fund, 1984  1984.1051.1
Sojka 3

*Morula II,* 1983–84
Lithograph printed in three colors on Japanese handmade Toyoshi paper (torn to size)
Sheet (irregular): $42\frac{1}{4}$ x $32\frac{1}{2}$ (107.3 x 82.6)
Signed (TW) and dated (1983–84), lower right
Numbered (30/37), lower left
Printers: Keith Brintzenhofe and Thomas Cox
Publisher: Universal Limited Art Editions (ULAE), West Islip, New York
Stewart S. MacDermott Fund, 1984  1984.1051.2
Sojka 4

*Morula III,* 1983–84
Lithograph printed in three colors with additions by hand in graphite
pencil on Japanese handmade Toyoshi paper (torn to size)
Sheet (irregular): 42 x 32$\frac{1}{2}$ (106.7 x 82.6)
Signed (TW) and dated (1983–84), upper right
Numbered (30/36), upper left
Printers: Keith Brintzenhofe and Thomas Cox
Publisher: Universal Limited Art Editions (ULAE), West Islip, New York
Stewart S. MacDermott Fund, 1984   1984.1051.3
Sojka 5

*Novalis,* 1983–89
Etching, open-bite etching, and aquatint printed in one color on Arches
En Tout Cas paper (torn to size)
Plate: 37$\frac{1}{4}$ x 26$\frac{3}{4}$ (94.6 x 67.9)
Sheet: 42$\frac{1}{2}$ x 31 (108 x 78.7)
Signed (Terry Winters) and dated (1983/1989), lower center
Numbered (18/50), lower left
Printers: Keith Brintzenhofe, John Lund, and Ji Hong Shi
Publisher: Universal Limited Art Editions (ULAE), West Islip, New York
Gift of Susan Sosnick, in memory of her husband, Robert Sosnick, 2001
2001.1.7
Sojka 48

*Double Standard,* 1984
Lithograph printed in twenty-two colors on Rolled Arches paper (torn to size)
Sheet (irregular): 78 x 42 (198.1 x 106.7)
Signed (TW) and dated (1984), lower right
Numbered (24/40), upper right
Printers: Keith Brintzenhofe, John Lund, and Douglas Volle
Publisher: Universal Limited Art Editions (ULAE), West Islip, New York
Gift of Susan Sosnick, in memory of her husband, Robert Sosnick, 2001
2001.1.3
Sojka 6

**Folio,** 1985–86
Portfolio of eleven lithographs printed in color
Sheets (irregular): 32 x 23 (81.3 x 58.4)
Signed (TW) in varying locations on each sheet
Dated (1985–1986), lower center of title page
Numbered (8/39), lower right of title page, following title
Printer: Keith Brintzenhofe
Publisher: Universal Limited Art Editions (ULAE), West Islip, New York
Gift of Susan Sosnick, in memory of her husband, Robert Sosnick, 2001

*Folio, Title Page*
Lithograph printed in fourteen colors on John Koller handmade paper
Signed (TW), lower center
2001.1.1a
Sojka 9

*Folio One*
Lithograph printed in six colors on J. Whatman paper
Signed (TW), lower right
2001.1.1c
Sojka 10

*Folio Two*
Lithograph printed in three colors on J. Whatman paper
Signed (TW), lower left
2001.1.1d
Sojka 11

*Folio Three*
Lithograph printed in four colors on J. Whatman paper
Signed (TW), upper right
2001.1.1e
Sojka 12

*Folio Four*
Lithograph printed in nine colors on J. Whatman paper
Signed (TW), lower right
2001.1.1f
Sojka 13

*Folio Five*
Lithograph printed in four colors on J. Whatman paper
Signed (TW), upper left
2001.1.1g
Sojka 14

*Folio Six*
Lithograph printed in six colors on J. Whatman paper
Signed (TW), lower right
2001.1.1h
Sojka 15

*Folio Seven*
Lithograph printed in thirteen colors on J. Whatman paper
Signed (TW), lower right
2001.1.1i
Sojka 16

*Folio Eight*
Lithograph printed in six colors on J. Whatman paper
Signed (TW), lower right
2001.1.1j
Sojka 17

*Folio Nine*
Lithograph printed in fifteen colors on J. Whatman paper
Signed (TW), lower right
2001.1.1k
Sojka 18

*Folio, Colophon*
Lithograph printed in twenty-three colors on John Koller handmade paper
Signed (TW), lower right
2001.1.1b
Sojka 19

## Fourteen Etchings, 1989

Portfolio of fourteen photogravures (lower plates) printed in one color on paper handmade in Amalfi, Italy (torn to size); separate hand-drawn Mylar gravures with various intaglio additions (upper plates) printed on Torinoko Gampi paper laid down on the Amalfi paper above the photogravures
Sheets (irregular): $18\frac{5}{8}$ x $14\frac{1}{8}$ (47.3 x 35.9)
Signed (Terry Winters), dated (1989), and numbered (AP 3/8), lower edge of cover
Signed (TW), upper right of each sheet
Printers: Keith Brintzenhofe, John Lund, and Hitoshi Kido, with assistance from Tina Diggs
Publisher: Universal Limited Art Editions (ULAE), West Islip, New York
Purchase, Reba and Dave Williams Gift, 1998

*Fourteen Etchings 1*
Hand-drawn Mylar gravure, sugar-lift aquatint, spit-bite aquatint, and scraper
Plate: 8 x $6\frac{1}{2}$ (20.3 x 16.5)
1998.83.1
Sojka 34

*Fourteen Etchings 2*
Hand-drawn Mylar gravure, spit-bite aquatint, and photogravure
Upper plate: 8 x $6\frac{5}{8}$ (20.3 x 16.8)
Lower plate: $5\frac{3}{8}$ x $3\frac{3}{4}$ (13.7 x 9.5)
1998.83.2
Sojka 35

*Fourteen Etchings 3*
Hand-drawn Mylar gravure, spit-bite aquatint, and photogravure
Upper plate: 8 x $6\frac{3}{4}$ (20.3 x 17.1)
Lower plate: 4 x 4 (10.2 x 10.2)
1998.83.3
Sojka 36

*Fourteen Etchings 4*
Hand-drawn Mylar gravure, spit-bite aquatint, and photogravure
Upper plate: 8 x $6\frac{1}{2}$ (20.3 x 16.5)
Lower plate: $5\frac{1}{2}$ x $3\frac{5}{8}$ (14 x 9.2)
1998.83.4
Sojka 37

*Fourteen Etchings 5*
Hand-drawn Mylar gravure, open-bite etching, and photogravure
Upper plate: $7\frac{7}{8}$ x $6\frac{5}{8}$ (20 x 16.8)
Lower plate: $3\frac{1}{2}$ x 4 (8.9 x 10.2)

1998.83.5
Sojka 38

*Fourteen Etchings 6*
Hand-drawn Mylar gravure, sugar-lift aquatint, and photogravure
Upper plate: $7\frac{7}{8}$ x $6\frac{1}{2}$ (20 x 16.5)
Lower plate: $3\frac{3}{4}$ x $3\frac{1}{4}$ (9.5 x 8.3)
1998.83.6
Sojka 39

*Fourteen Etchings 7*
Hand-drawn Mylar gravure, spit-bite aquatint, and photogravure
Upper plate: 8 x $6\frac{3}{4}$ (20.3 x 17.1)
Lower plate: $3\frac{5}{8}$ x $2\frac{1}{2}$ (9.2 x 6.4)
1998.83.7
Sojka 40

*Fourteen Etchings 8*
Hand-drawn Mylar gravure, spit-bite aquatint, and photogravure
Upper plate: 8 x $6\frac{5}{8}$ (20.3 x 16.8)
Lower plate: 5 x $2\frac{5}{8}$ (12.7 x 6.7)
1998.83.8
Sojka 41

*Fourteen Etchings 9*
Hand-drawn Mylar gravure, sugar-lift aquatint, spit-bite aquatint, and photogravure
Upper plate: 8 x $6\frac{5}{8}$ (20.3 x 16.8)
Lower plate: $4\frac{1}{8}$ x $3\frac{1}{8}$ (10.5 x 7.9)
1998.83.9
Sojka 42

*Fourteen Etchings 10*
Hand-drawn Mylar gravure, soft-ground etching, spit-bite aquatint, and photogravure
Upper plate: $8\frac{1}{8}$ x $6\frac{7}{8}$ (20.6 x 17.5)
Lower plate: $5\frac{1}{4}$ x $3\frac{5}{8}$ (13.3 x 9.2)
1998.83.10
Sojka 43

*Fourteen Etchings 11*
Hand-drawn Mylar gravure, spit-bite aquatint, and photogravure
Upper plate: 8 x $6\frac{3}{4}$ (20.3 x 17.1)
Lower plate: $5\frac{1}{2}$ x $3\frac{7}{8}$ (14 x 9.8)
1998.83.11
Sojka 44

*Fourteen Etchings 12*
Hand-drawn Mylar gravure, spit-bite aquatint, and photogravure
Upper plate: 8 x $6\frac{5}{8}$ (20.3 x 16.8)
Lower plate: 5 x $3\frac{1}{2}$ (12.7 x 8.9)
1998.83.12
Sojka 45

*Fourteen Etchings 13*
Hand-drawn Mylar gravure, open-bite etching, and photogravure
Upper plate: $7\frac{7}{8}$ x $6\frac{1}{2}$ (20 x 16.5)
Lower plate: $5\frac{3}{8}$ x $3\frac{1}{2}$ (13.7 x 8.9)
1998.83.13
Sojka 46

*Fourteen Etchings 14*
Hand-drawn Mylar gravure, spit-bite aquatint, and photogravure
Upper plate: 8 x $6\frac{5}{8}$ (20.3 x 16.8)
Lower plate: $5\frac{1}{2}$ x $2\frac{3}{4}$ (14 x 7)
1998.83.14
Sojka 47

**Furrows,** 1989
Portfolio of five woodcuts printed in one color on CartaLafranca paper
issued in a handmade three-page paper folder
Blocks: $25\frac{3}{8}$ x $19\frac{1}{2}$ (64.5 x 49.5)
Sheets (irregular): $26\frac{1}{2}$ x $21\frac{1}{4}$ (67.3 x 54)
Signed (Terry Winters) and numbered (25/45), lower left of each sheet
Printer: François Lafranca, Versico, Switzerland
Publisher: Peter Blum Edition, New York
Purchase, Reba and Dave Williams Gift, 1998

*Furrows,* title page of the handmade paper folder
1998.5.1a

*Furrows I*
1998.5.2
Sojka 49

*Furrows II*
1998.5.3
Sojka 50

*Furrows III*
1998.5.4
Sojka 51

*Furrows IV*
1998.5.5
Sojka 52

*Furrows V*
1998.5.6
Sojka 53

*Section,* 1991
Lithograph printed in four colors on Torinoko paper
Sheet: $59\frac{1}{2}$ x 40 (151.1 x 101.6)
Signed (Terry Winters) and dated (1991), upper center
Numbered (18/68), upper right
Printers: Keith Brintzenhofe and Douglas Volle
Publisher: Universal Limited Art Editions (ULAE), West Islip, New York

Gift of Susan Sosnick, in memory of her husband, Robert Sosnick, 2001
2001.1.8
Sojka 57

**Field Notes,** 1992
Portfolio of twenty-five intaglio prints printed in one color on
Hahnemühle paper
Plates: $8\frac{1}{2}$ x $6\frac{1}{4}$ (21.6 x 15.9)
Sheets: 13 x 10 (33 x 25.4)
Signed (Terry Winters), lower left of each sheet
Numbered (33/75), lower right of each sheet
Printer: Atelier Aldo Crommelynck, Paris
Publisher: Aldo Crommelynck, Paris
John B. Turner Fund, 1992

*Field Notes, 1*
Etching and spit-bite aquatint
1992.1063.1
Sojka 71

*Field Notes, 2*
Sugar-lift aquatint, spit-bite aquatint, open-bite etching, and scraper
1992.1063.2
Sojka 72

*Field Notes, 3*
Etching
1992.1063.3
Sojka 73

*Field Notes, 4*
Open-bite etching and spit-bite aquatint
1992.1063.4
Sojka 74

*Field Notes, 5*
Soft-ground etching
1992.1063.5
Sojka 75

*Field Notes, 12*
Etching, sugar-lift aquatint, and spit-bite aquatint
1992.1063.12
Sojka 82

*Field Notes, 19*
Sugar-lift aquatint, spit-bite aquatint, and open-bite etching
1992.1063.19
Sojka 89

*Field Notes, 21*
Etching
1992.1063.21
Sojka 91

*Field Notes, 22*
Sugar-lift aquatint, spit-bite aquatint, and open-bite etching
1992.1063.22
Sojka 92

*Field Notes, 24*
Soft-ground etching and spit-bite aquatint
1992.1063.24
Sojka 94


## Models for Synthetic Pictures, 1994
Portfolio of twelve intaglio prints each combining open-bite etching, soft-ground etching, sugar-lift aquatint, and spit-bite aquatint printed in five colors on Gampi paper laid down on Lana Gravure paper (torn to size) with a three-page Lana Gravure paper folder comprising a title page (with black type on a solid blue rectangle), a page with text by Terry Winters (with black type on a solid red rectangle), and a colophon page (with black type on a solid yellow rectangle)
Plates: $13\frac{1}{2}$ x $16\frac{1}{2}$ (34.3 x 41.9)
Sheets (irregular): $19\frac{3}{8}$ x $22\frac{1}{4}$ (49.2 x 56.5)
Signed (Terry Winters) and dated (1994), lower right of each sheet
Numbered (21/35), lower left of each sheet
Printers: Hitoshi Kido, John Lund, Nancy Mesenbourg, and Ji Hong Shi
Publisher: Universal Limited Art Editions (ULAE), West Islip, New York
Gift of Susan Sosnick, in memory of her husband, Robert Sosnick, 2001

*Models for Synthetic Pictures, 1*
2001.1.2a
Sojka 97

*Models for Synthetic Pictures, 2*
2001.1.2b
Sojka 98

*Models for Synthetic Pictures, 3*
2001.1.2c
Sojka 99

*Models for Synthetic Pictures, 4*
2001.1.2d
Sojka 100

*Models for Synthetic Pictures, 5*
2001.1.2e
Sojka 101

*Models for Synthetic Pictures, 6*
2001.1.2f
Sojka 102

*Models for Synthetic Pictures, 7*
2001.1.2g
Sojka 103

*Models for Synthetic Pictures, 8*
2001.1.2h
Sojka 104

*Models for Synthetic Pictures, 9*
2001.1.2i
Sojka 105

*Models for Synthetic Pictures, 10*
2001.1.2j
Sojka 106

*Models for Synthetic Pictures, 11*
2001.1.2k
Sojka 107

*Models for Synthetic Pictures, 12*
2001.1.2l
Sojka 108


## Glyphs, 1995
Portfolio of six linoleum cuts printed in one color on Sekishu paper hand-dyed with indigo
Sheets (irregular): $24\frac{1}{8}$ x $17\frac{3}{8}$ (61.3 x 44.1)
Signed (Terry Winters), lower left of each sheet
Numbered (16/27), lower center of each sheet
Printer: Leslie Miller
Publisher: The Grenfell Press, New York
Purchase, Reba and Dave Williams Gift, 1998

*Glyphs, 1*
Block: $22\frac{7}{8}$ x $16\frac{7}{8}$ (58.1 x 42.9)
1998.82.1
Sojka 110

*Glyphs, 2*
Block: $22\frac{3}{4}$ x $16\frac{7}{8}$ (57.8 x 42.9)
1998.82.2
Sojka 111

*Glyphs, 3*
Block: $22\frac{7}{8}$ x $16\frac{1}{4}$ (58.1 x 41.3)
1998.82.3
Sojka 112

*Glyphs, 4*
Block: $22\frac{7}{8}$ x $16\frac{7}{8}$ (58.1 x 42.9)
1998.82.4
Sojka 113

*Glyphs, 5*
Block: $22\frac{7}{8}$ x $16\frac{7}{8}$ (58.1 x 42.9)
1998.82.5
Sojka 114

*Glyphs, 6*
Block: 22¾ x 16 (57.8 x 40.6)
1998.82.6
Sojka 115

*Systems Diagram,* 1996
Etching, soft-ground etching, and sugar-lift aquatint printed in one color
on Arches En Tout Cas paper (torn to size)
Plate: 33¾ x 42¼ (85.7 x 107.3)
Sheet: 42 x 50 (106.7 x 127)
Signed (Terry Winters) and dated (1996), upper right
Numbered (4/18), upper left
Printers: Lorena Salcedo-Watson, Scott Smith, and Craig Zammiello
Publisher: Universal Limited Art Editions (ULAE), West Islip, New York
Purchase, Reba and Dave Williams Gift, 1998   1998.81
Sojka 118

**Graphic Primitives,** 1998
Portfolio of nine woodcuts printed in one color on Japanese Kochi paper
rinsed with ink
Blocks: 18 x 24 (45.7 x 61)
Sheets (irregular): 20 x 26 (50.8 x 66)
Signed (Terry Winters) and dated (1998), lower right of each sheet
Numbered (TP), lower left of each sheet
Printers: David Lasry, Pedro Barbeito, and Guy Corriero
Publisher: Two Palms Press, New York, and Terry Winters
Gift of Susan Sosnick, in memory of her husband, Robert Sosnick, 2001

*Graphic Primitives, 1*
2001.1.4a
Sojka 123

*Graphic Primitives, 2*
2001.1.4b
Sojka 124

*Graphic Primitives, 3*
2001.1.4c
Sojka 125

*Graphic Primitives, 4*
2001.1.4d
Sojka 126

*Graphic Primitives, 5*
2001.1.4e
Sojka 127

*Graphic Primitives, 6*
2001.1.4f
Sojka 128

*Graphic Primitives, 7*
2001.1.4g
Sojka 129

*Graphic Primitives, 8*
2001.1.4h
Sojka 130

*Graphic Primitives, 9*
2001.1.4i
Sojka 131

*Internal and External Values,* 1998
Sugar-lift aquatint and open-bite etching printed in one color on Arches
En Tout Cas paper (torn to size)
Plate: 33½ x 42½ (85.1 x 108)
Sheet: 42 x 49¾ (106.7 x 126.4)
Signed (Terry Winters) and dated (1998), lower right
Numbered (4/35), lower left
Printers: Lorena Salcedo-Watson, Ji Hong Shi, and Craig Zammiello
Publisher: Universal Limited Art Editions (ULAE), West Islip,
New York
Gift of Susan Sosnick, in memory of her husband, Robert Sosnick, 2001
2001.1.6
Sojka 132

*Multiple Visualization Technique,* 1998
Sugar-lift aquatint and open-bite etching printed in four colors on Arches
En Tout Cas paper (torn to size)
Plate: 43¾ x 33¾ (111.1 x 85.7)
Sheet: 53 x 43 (134.6 x 109.2)
Signed (Terry Winters) and dated (1998), lower right
Numbered (4/41), lower left
Printers: Ji Hong Shi and Craig Zammiello
Publisher: Universal Limited Art Editions (ULAE), West Islip, New York
Gift of Susan Sosnick, in memory of her husband, Robert Sosnick, 2001
2001.1.5
Sojka 144

**Set of Ten,** 1998
Portfolio of ten intaglio prints combining Xerox transfer, open-bite
etching, spit-bite aquatint, and sugar-lift aquatint printed in one color
on paper handmade in England
Plates: 13¾ x 10⅞ (34.9 x 27.6)
Sheets: 18¾ x 15 (47.6 x 38.1)
Signed (TWinters), lower right of each sheet
Numbered (6/38), lower left of each sheet
Printers: Doug Bennett, Ji Hong Shi, and Craig Zammiello
Publisher: Universal Limited Art Editions (ULAE), West Islip, New York
Purchase, Reba and Dave Williams Gift, 2001

2001.52a

Sojka 134

2001.52b

Sojka 135

2001.52c

Sojka 136

2001.52d

Sojka 137

2001.52e

Sojka 138

2001.52f

Sojka 139

2001.52g

Sojka 140

2001.52h

Sojka 141

2001.52i

Sojka 142

2001.52j

Sojka 143

*Untitled (Lincoln Center),* 1999*

Screenprint printed in fourteen colors on 300 g Somerset paper

Sheet: $38\frac{1}{8}$ x $49\frac{1}{8}$ (96.8 x 124.8)

Signed (Terry Winters), dated (1999), and numbered (AP 8/18), lower left

Embossed with printer's blindstamp (X), lower right

Edition: 108 plus 18 AP, 9 PP

Proofs: 2 BAT, 10 unsigned replacements, 1 TP

Printers: Brand X Editions, New York (Roberto Mercedes, Luis Vasquez, and Steve Sangenario)

Publisher: Lincoln Center for the Performing Arts, New York/List Art Posters

Colors: Nine shades of cobalt blue and five shades of black

Printing sequence: Printed on a hand-fed Viking semiautomatic silkscreen press; 1–4) cobalt  5–8) black  9–13) cobalt  14) black

Gift of the artist, 2001  2001.3.1

*Amplitude,* 2000

Sugar-lift aquatint and open-bite etching printed in four colors on Arches En Tout Cas paper (torn to size)

Plate: $42\frac{1}{2}$ x $33\frac{1}{2}$ (108 x 85.1)

Sheet: $53\frac{3}{8}$ x $43\frac{1}{2}$ (135.6 x 110.5)

Signed (Terry Winters) and dated (2000), lower right

Numbered (25/45), lower left

Embossed with publisher's blindstamp (ULAE), lower left

Edition: 45 plus 11 AP, 4 PP

Proofs: 1 BAT, 1 signing proof, 1 TP

Printers: Doug Bennett, Nancy Mesenbourg, and Craig Zammiello

Publisher: Universal Limited Art Editions (ULAE), Bayshore, New York

Colors: Ocher, brown, black, and blue

Printing sequence: Four printings from four plates on an etching press; 1) ocher  2) brown  3) black  4) blue

Gift of Robert and Lynda Shapiro, 2001  2001.2.1

*Linking Graphics,* 2000

Sugar-lift aquatint and open-bite etching printed in two colors on Arches En Tout Cas paper (torn to size)

Plate: $33\frac{3}{4}$ x $42\frac{3}{4}$ (85.7 x 108.6)

Sheet: $40\frac{1}{4}$ x 49 (102.2 x 124.5)

Signed (Terry Winters) and dated (2000), lower right

Numbered (27/34), lower left

Embossed with publisher's blindstamp (ULAE), lower left

Edition: 34 plus 9 AP, 4 PP

Proofs: 3 TP

Printers: Doug Bennett, Brian Berry, Ji Hong Shi, and Craig Zammiello

Publisher: Universal Limited Art Editions (ULAE), Bayshore, New York

Colors: Gray and black

Printing sequence: Two printings from two plates on an etching press; 1) gray  2) black

Gift of Robert and Lynda Shapiro, 2001  2001.2.2

*Location Plan,* 2000*

Single-color screenprint in black printed on Clearprint fade-out cotton vellum graph paper

Sheet: 41 x $54\frac{3}{8}$ (104.1 x 138.1)

Signed (Terry Winters), dated (2000), and numbered (Location Plan 99/100), lower left

Edition: 100 plus 10 AP, 6 PP

Proofs: 1 BAT, 4 TP

Printers: Brand X Editions, New York (Roberto Mercedes, Luis Vasquez, and Steve Sangenario)

Publisher: IC Editions, New York

Color: Black

Printing sequence: Printed on a hand-fed Viking semiautomatic silkscreen press

Gift of the artist, 2001  2001.3.2

*Untitled (Trisha Brown Dance Co.),* 2000*
Lithograph printed in three colors on a hand-fed offset press on J. Green paper
Sheet: 22¾ x 42⅞ (57.8 x 108.9)
Signed (Terry Winters) and dated (2000), lower right
Numbered (21/25), lower left
Embossed with publisher's blindstamp (ULAE), lower left
Edition: 25 plus 9 AP, 3 PP
Proofs: 1 BAT
Printers: Doug Bennett, Douglas Volle, and Bruce Wankel
Publisher: Universal Limited Art Editions (ULAE), Bayshore, New York
Colors: Black, graphite, and blue
Printing sequence: Three printings from three plates on a hand-fed offset lithography press; 1) black  2) graphite  3) blue
Gift of Robert and Lynda Shapiro, 2001  2001.2.3

*Cluster,* 2001*
Photogravure, sugar-lift aquatint, and open-bite etching printed in three colors on Somerset Textured paper (torn to size)
Plate: 23¾ x 19¾ (60.3 x 50.2)
Sheet: 33¾ x 27¾ (85.7 x 70.5)
Signed (Terry Winters) and dated (2001), lower right
Numbered (AP 7/20), lower left
Embossed with publisher's blindstamp (ULAE), lower left
Edition: 50 plus 20 AP, 3 PP
Proofs: 1 BAT, 6 TP, 3 WP
Printers: Doug Bennett, Brian Berry, and Craig Zammiello
Publisher: Universal Limited Art Editions (ULAE), Bayshore, New York
Colors: Blue and black
Printing sequence: Three printings from three plates on an etching press; 1) Prussian blue  2) cobalt blue  3) blue/black
Gift of the artist, 2001  2001.200.1

*Pattern,* 2001
Color inkjet and offset lithograph printed on Somerset Textured paper
Plate: 52 x 39¾ (132.1 x 101)

Sheet: 54½ x 40⅛ (138.4 x 101.9)
Signed (Terry Winters) and dated (2001), upper right
Numbered (AP 7/10), upper left
Embossed with publisher's blindstamp (ULAE), lower left
Edition: 38 plus 10 AP, 3 PP
Proofs: 1 BAT, 2 TP
Printers: Douglas Volle, Bruce Wankel, and Vanessa Viola
Publisher: Universal Limited Art Editions (ULAE), Bayshore, New York
Colors: Color inkjet and black
Printing sequence: Two printings, one on a six-color Roland inkjet and one plate on a hand-fed offset lithography press; 1) color inkjet 2) black
Gift of the artist, 2001  2001.200.2


*Perfection, Way, Origin,* 2001
Bound book containing a translated text by Jean Starobinski and twenty-eight etchings by Terry Winters, issued with the *Set of Ten* portfolio (see pages 36–37) and a bound copy of the original French text, all in an aluminum box
Book (closed): 18⅞ x 15 x 2 (47.9 x 38.1 x 5.1). English text trans. Richard Pevear. Typeset in 36 pt. Perpetua Mau by Richard Hunt, Archetype, Toronto, and printed on Lana Gravure paper on a hand-fed letterpress. Signed by the author and signed, dated, and numbered by the artist on the colophon page. Embossed with the publisher's blindstamp (ULAE), lower left of colophon page. 58 pages
Bound original French text: Typeset in 13 pt. Perpetua Mau and printed on Lana Gravure paper on a hand-fed offset lithography press
Book and box designed by Terry Winters and Bruce Mau with Barr Gilmore, Bruce Mau Design, Toronto; bindings and folder created by Claudia Cohen using handmade UICB paper; box constructed by the Aluminium Case Company, London
Edition: 38 plus 9 AP, 6 PP
Printers: Doug Bennett, Nancy Mesenbourg, Lorena Salcedo-Watson, Ji Hong Shi, Douglas Volle, Bruce Wankel, and Craig Zammiello
Publisher: Universal Limited Art Editions (ULAE), Bayshore, New York
Purchase, Reba and Dave Williams Gift, 2001

# Selected Bibliography

**Books and Exhibition Catalogues**

Adams, Brooks, and Lisa Liebmann. *Young Americans 2: New American Art at the Saatchi Gallery*. Exhibition catalogue. London: Saatchi Gallery, 1998.

Amalfitano, Lelia, and Raphael Rubinstein. *Terry Winters: Recent Works*. Exhibition catalogue. Boston: School of the Museum of Fine Arts, 1997.

Gilbert-Rolfe, Jeremy. *Jasper Johns, Brice Marden, Terry Winters: Drawings*. Exhibition catalogue. Los Angeles: Margo Leavin Gallery, 1992.

Goldman, Judith. *Three Printmakers: Jennifer Bartlett, Susan Rothenberg, Terry Winters*. Exhibition brochure. New York: Whitney Museum of American Art, 1986.

Juncosa, Enrique, and Ronald Jones. *Terry Winters*. Exhibition catalogue. London: Whitechapel Art Gallery; Valencia: Institut Valencia d'Art Modern, 1998.

Kertess, Klaus, and Martin Kunz. *Terry Winters*. Exhibition catalogue. Lucerne: Kunstmuseum Luzern, 1985.

Lewison, Jeremy. *Terry Winters: Eight Paintings*. Exhibition catalogue. London: Tate Gallery, 1986.

Liebmann, Lisa. *Terry Winters: Index I–X*. Exhibition catalogue. Tokyo: Gallery Mukai, 1989.

Phillips, Lisa. *Terry Winters*. Exhibition catalogue. New York: Whitney Museum of American Art, 1991.

Plous, Phyllis, and Christopher Knight. *Terry Winters: Painting and Drawing*. Exhibition catalogue. Santa Barbara: University Art Museum, University of California, Santa Barbara, 1987.

Rajchman, John, and Ronald Jones. *Terry Winters: Graphic Primitives*. Exhibition catalogue. New York: Matthew Marks Gallery, 1999.

Schulz-Hoffman, Carla. *Sieben Amerikanische Maler*. Exhibition catalogue. Munich: Bayerische Staatsgemäldesammlungen, Staatsgalerie Moderner Kunst München, 1991.

Sebald, W. G. *Terry Winters*. Exhibition catalogue. Basel: Kunsthalle Basel, 2000.

Semff, Michael. *Terry Winters: Foundations and Systems. Fünfzig Neue Zeichnungen von Terry Winters/Fifty New Drawings by Terry Winters*. Exhibition catalogue. Munich: Galerie Fred Jahn, 1995.

Shapiro, David. *Terry Winters: Fourteen Drawings/Fourteen Etchings*. Exhibition catalogue. Munich: Galerie Jahn und Fusban, 1990.

Sojka, Nancy, with Nancy Watson Barr. *Terry Winters Prints 1982–1998: A Catalogue Raisonné*. Detroit: The Detroit Institute of Arts, 1999.

Weinberg, Adam D. *Aldo Crommelynck: Master Prints with American Artists*. Exhibition brochure. New York: Whitney Museum of American Art at Equitable Center, 1988.

Winters, Terry. *Intersections and Animations: 50 Drawings*. New York: Dome Editions, 1999.

Winters, Terry. *Ocular Proofs*. New York: The Grenfell Press, 1995.

Winters, Terry, and Adam Fuss. *Terry Winters: Computation of Chains*. Exhibition catalogue. New York: Matthew Marks Gallery, 1997.

Winters, Terry, and Roberta Smith. *Schema*. West Islip, New York: Universal Limited Art Editions, 1988.

**Periodicals**

Ackley, Clifford S. "'Double Standard': The Prints of Terry Winters." *The Print Collector's Newsletter* 18, no. 4 (September–October 1987), pp. 121–24.

——. "Terry Winters and Cliff Ackley: A Conversation." *Art New England* 14 (June–July 1993), pp. 29–31.

Adams, Brooks. "Terry Winters at Sonnabend." *Art in America* 82, no. 10 (October 1994), pp. 130–31.

Cooke, Lynne. "Terry Winters' Poetic Conceits." *Artscribe International*, no. 59 (September–October 1986), pp. 62–64.

Green, Roger. "Robert and Susan Sosnick: A Marriage of Taste." *Art News* 96 (April 1997), pp. 101–04.

Hughes, Robert. "Art: Obliquely Addressing Nature." *Time,* February 24, 1986, p. 83.

Liebmann, Lisa. "Terry Winters, Sonnabend Gallery." *Artforum* 21, no. 6 (February 1983), p. 72.

Princenthal, Nancy. "Artists Book Beat." *The Print Collector's Newsletter* 27, no. 2 (May–June 1996), pp. 67–69.

**Newspaper Articles**

Brenson, Michael. "Review: Sonnabend Gallery." *The New York Times,* February 21, 1986.

Cotter, Holland. "Terry Winters Drawings." *The New York Times,* May 12, 1995.

Kimmelman, Michael. "Cells, Crystals, Bugs and Shells, Rendered in Paint." *The New York Times,* March 8, 1992.

——. "Terry Winters." *The New York Times,* October 31, 1997.

Knight, Christopher. "Winters' Growth: Sensual Fusion of Culture and Nature." *The Los Angeles Times,* September 18, 1991.

Schjeldahl, Peter. "The Redeemer." *The Village Voice,* October 28, 1997.

Wallach, Amei. "Picturing the Painting Process." *Newsday,* February 28, 1986.